STRUM IT GUITAR

AUTHENTIC CHORDS
ORIGINAL KEYS
COMPLETE SONGS

Carole King COLLECTION

Arranged by Mick O'Brien
Photo by Maryanne Bilham

ISBN 0-634-01559-1

HAL•LEONARD®
CORPORATION

7777 W. BLUEMOUND RD. P.O. BOX 13819 MILWAUKEE, WI 53213

Visit Hal Leonard Online at
www.halleonard.com

HOW TO USE THIS BOOK

Strum It is the series designed especially to get you playing (and singing!) along with your favorite songs. The idea is simple—the songs are arranged using their original keys in lead sheet format, giving you the chords for each song, beginning to end. The melody and lyrics are also shown to help you keep your spot and sing along.

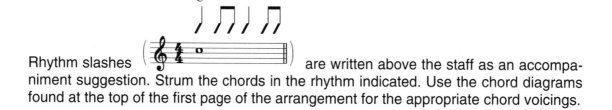

Rhythm slashes are written above the staff as an accompaniment suggestion. Strum the chords in the rhythm indicated. Use the chord diagrams found at the top of the first page of the arrangement for the appropriate chord voicings.

Additional Musical Definitions

⊓	• Downstroke
∨	• Upstroke
D.S. al Coda	• Go back to the sign (𝄋), then play until the measure marked *"To Coda,"* then skip to the section labelled *"Coda."*
D.C. al Fine	• Go back to the beginning of the song and play until the measure marked *"Fine"* (end).
cont. rhy. sim.	• Continue using similar rhythm pattern.
N.C.	• Instrument is silent (drops out).
𝄆 𝄇	• Repeat measures between signs.
1. 2.	• When a repeated section has different endings, play the first ending only the first time and the second ending only the second time.

Been to Canaan

Words and Music by Carole King

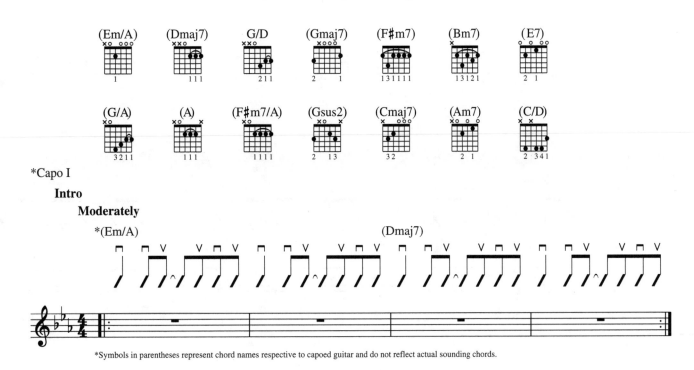

*Capo I

Intro

Moderately

*Symbols in parentheses represent chord names respective to capoed guitar and do not reflect actual sounding chords.

Verse

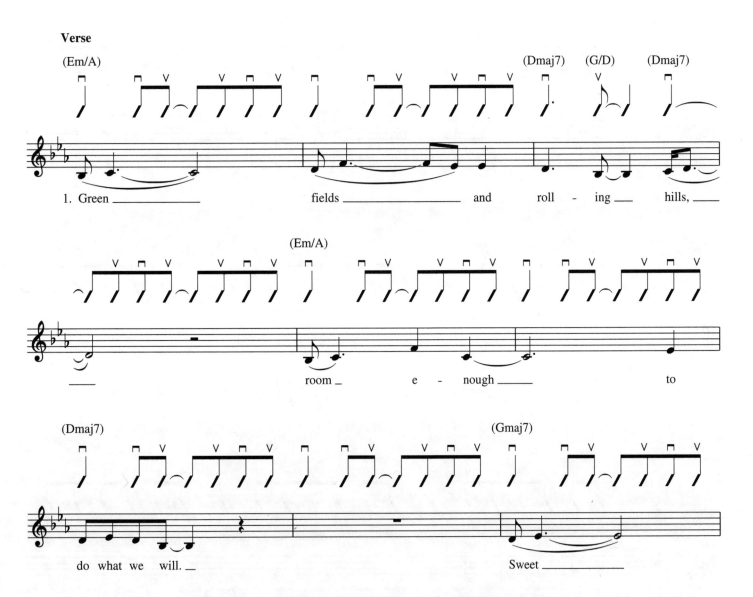

1. Green _____ fields _____ and roll - ing _____ hills, _____ _____ room _ e - nough _____ to do what we will. _ Sweet _____

(F#m7)

dreams _____ of yes - ter - time __ are

(Bm7)　　　　　　　　　　　(E7)　　　　　　　　　　　(G/A)

run - nin' through _ my mind _____ of a place __ I left __ be - hind.

%. **Chorus**

(A)　　　　　　　　　　　(Gmaj7)

__ { 1., 3. Been / 2. been } so _____ long _____ I ____

(Dmaj7)　　　　　　　　　　　　　　　　　　(G/A)

can't re - mem - ber __ when, __ { 1., 2. I've / 3. but I've } been to Ca - naan and I

(Dmaj7)

want to go back __ a - gain. __

Been so _____ long. _____ I'm liv - in' till then, __

{ 1., 2. 'cause I've }
{ 3. I've } been to Ca - naan and a I won't rest __ un - til

To Coda 2 ⊕   *To Coda 1* ⊕

I ____ go ___ back _____ a - gain.

Verse

2. Though _____ I'm _____ con - tent with my - self, __

some - times _____ I _____ long _____ to be

5

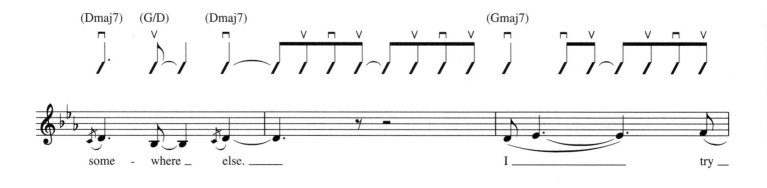

some - where _ else. _____   I _____ try _

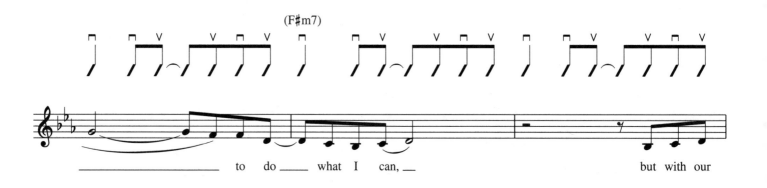

_____ to do _ what I can, _   but with our

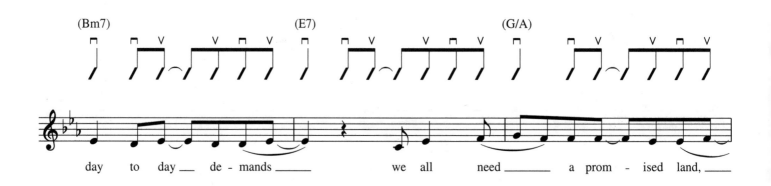

day to day _ de - mands _____   we all   need _____ a prom - ised land, _____

D.S. al Coda 1   ⊕ **Coda 1**

Bridge

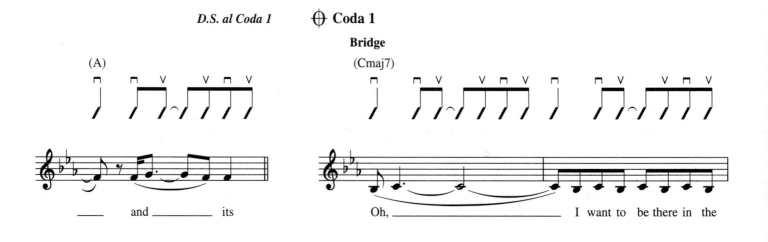

_____ and _____ its   Oh, _____ I want to be there in the

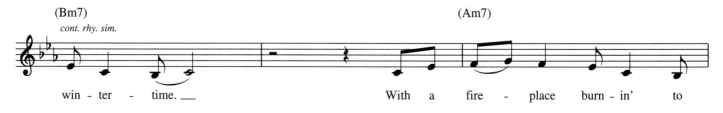

win - ter - time. _   With a fire - place burn - in' to

warm   me,   and   you _____ to   hold ___ me   when it's

D.S. al Coda 2   ⊕ **Coda 2**

Outro

(G/A)   (Gsus2)

storm - y. _____   gain.

(G/A)   (F♯m7/A)

I've   been   to   Ca - naan and a   I won't   rest___   un – til

(G/A) (F♯m7/A) (Em/A)   (Gsus2)

I ___   go ___   back _____   a - gain.

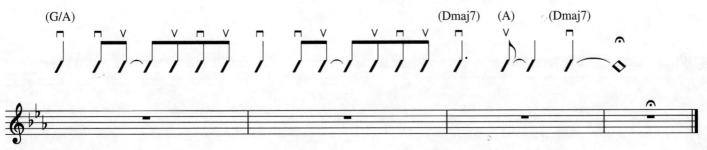

(G/A)   (Dmaj7) (A)   (Dmaj7)

Believe in Humanity

Words and Music by Carole King

Chorus

- ing. ___ But don't tell _ me _ a - bout the things you've _ heard, _

may - be I'm wrong, _____ but I want to be - lieve _____ in hu - man -

- i - ty. ___

Verse

2. I know it's of - ten true, sad to say, ___

we have been un - kind to one an - oth - er. ___ Tell me, how man - y times _ has the

gold - en rule _ been ap - plied by man _ to his broth - er? Well, I be -

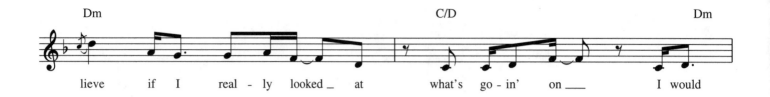

Dm .... C/D .... Dm

lieve if I real - ly looked _ at what's go - in' on ___ I would

Chorus

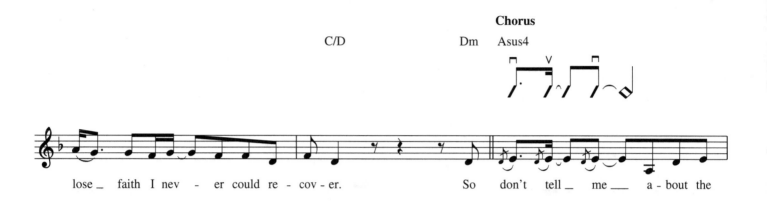

C/D .... Dm Asus4

lose _ faith I nev - er could re - cov - er. So don't tell _ me _ a - bout the

C7sus4 .... Fmaj7

things you've _ heard, ___ may - be I'm wrong _ but I want to be - lieve _

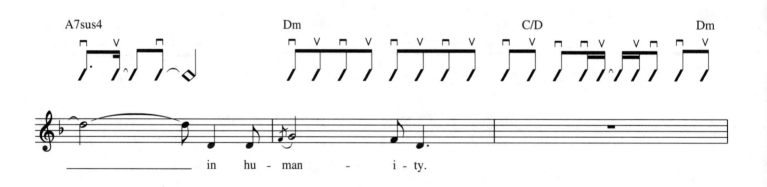

A7sus4 .... Dm .... C/D .... Dm

_____ in hu - man - i - ty.

Interlude

C/D .... Dm .... C/D .... Dm

Brother, Brother

Words and Music by Carole King

broth - er, broth - er, broth - er.

Verse

1. I've been watch - in' ev - 'ry - thing __ you __ do, __
2. *See additional lyrics*

and I've been a wish - ing __ on - ly good for __ you. __

All you've got __ to do __ is just to want __ it __ too, __ and it's

gon - na come, __ it's gon - na come __ to you. __

Chorus

Ooh, _____ broth - er, broth - er, broth - er. _____

I know you've _ been a hang - in' on _ a long _ time. _____ { But I / You know I }

love _____ you, love you, love you like no _____ oth - er. Oh, _____

To Coda ⊕

_____ broth - er, broth - er, { broth - er of mine. _____ / broth - er, broth - er, broth - er. }

Interlude

14

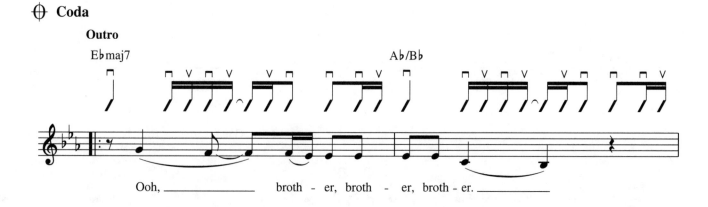

Additional Lyrics

2. You have always been so good to me,
   And though you didn't always talk to me,
   There wasn't much my lovin' eyes could not see.
   And I don't believe you need all your misery.

Corazón

Words and Music by Carole King

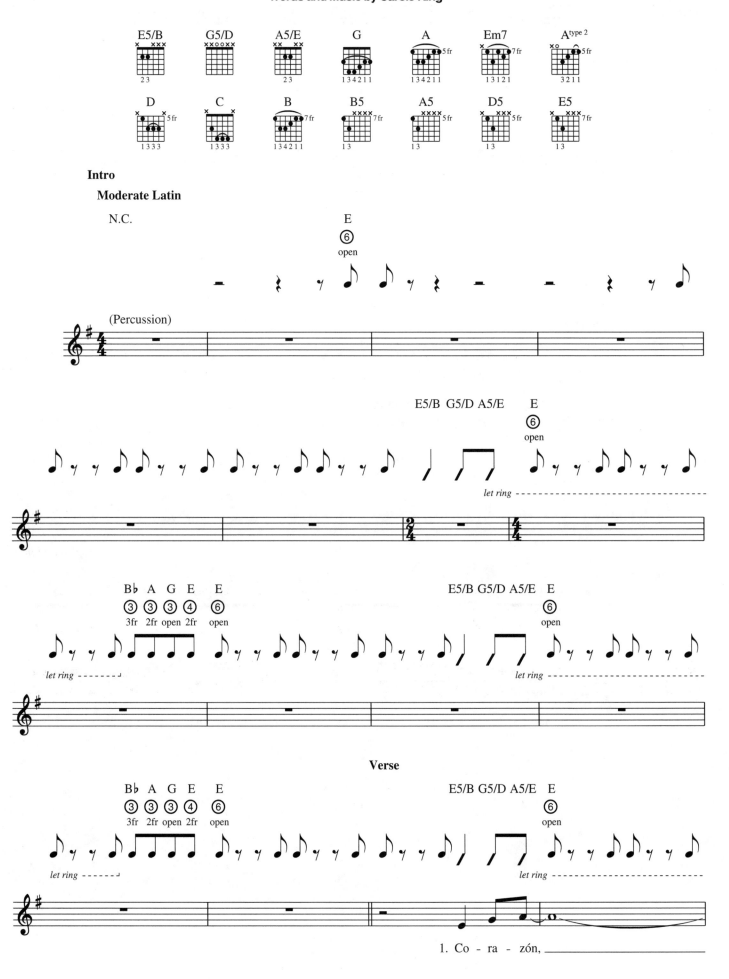

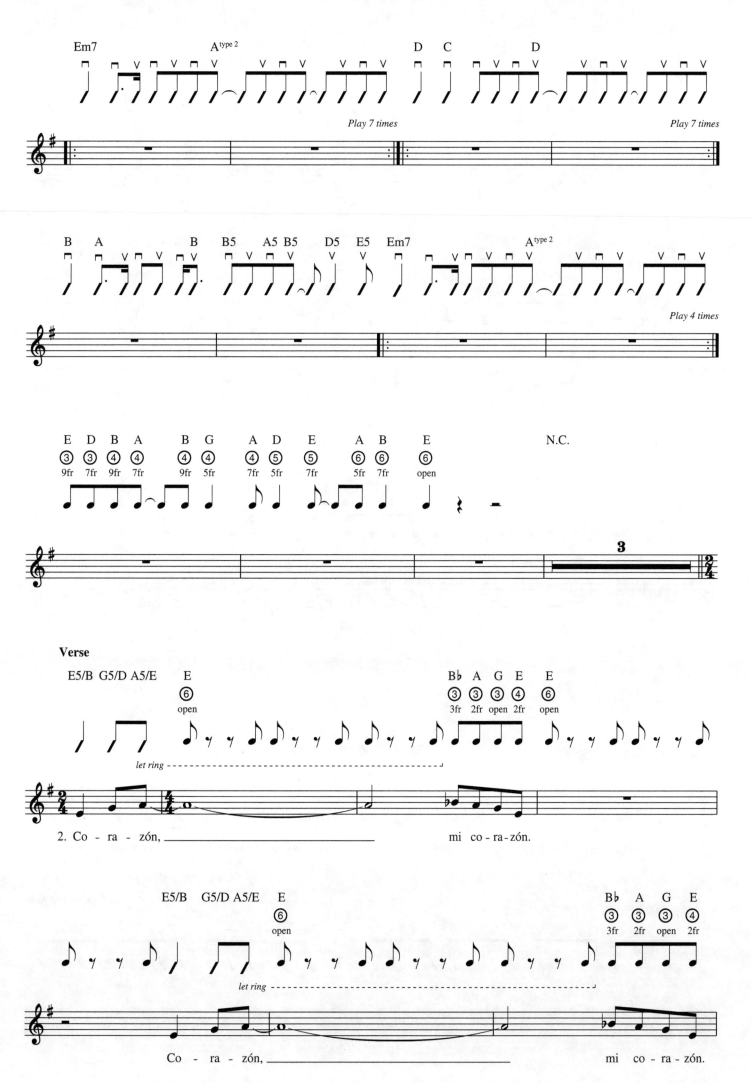

2. Co - ra - zón, _____ mi co - ra - zón.

Co - ra - zón, _____ mi co - ra - zón.

(You Make Me Feel Like)
A Natural Woman

Words and Music by Gerry Goffin, Carole King and Jerry Wexler

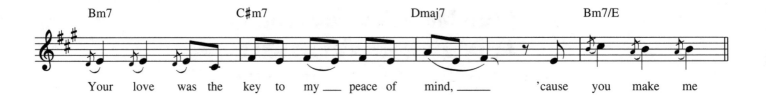

Bm7   C♯m7   Dmaj7   Bm7/E

Your love was the key to my ___ peace of mind, ___ 'cause you make me

Chorus

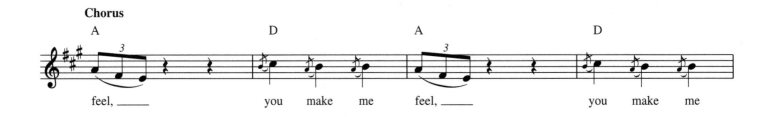

A   D   A   D

feel, ___ you make me feel, ___ you make me

1.

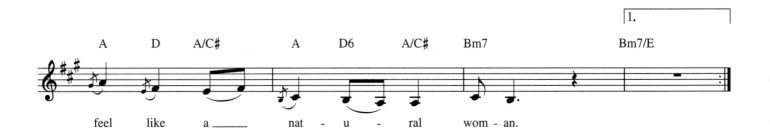

A D A/C♯   A D6 A/C♯ Bm7   Bm7/E

feel like a ___ nat - u - ral wom - an.

2.   **Bridge**

Bm7/E   A   G/A   D

Oh, ___ ba - by, what you've done to ___ me! ___ (What you've done to me!)

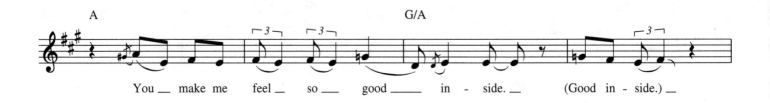

A   G/A

You ___ make me feel ___ so ___ good ___ in - side. ___ (Good in - side.) ___

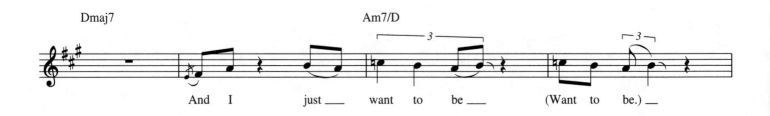

Dmaj7   Am7/D

And I just ___ want to be ___ (Want to be.) ___

D   A/C♯   Bm7   Bm7/E

close to you. You make me feel ___ so a - live! ___ You ___ make me

Outro

Additional Lyrics

2. Oh, when my soul was in the lost and found,
   You came along to claim it.
   I didn't know just what was wrong with me,
   'Till your kiss helped me name it.
   Now I'm no longer doubtful of what I'm livin' for,
   'Cause if I make ya happy I don't need to do more.
   You make me feel,...

Hi-De-Ho
(That Old Sweet Roll)

Words and Music by Gerry Goffin and Carole King

Gon - na get me a piece of the sky. _____ Gon - na find me some of that

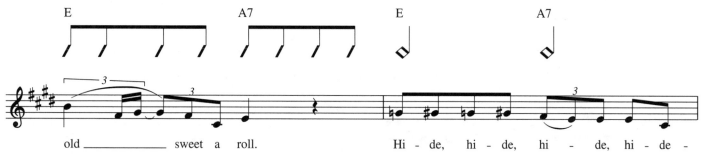

old _____ sweet a roll. Hi - de, hi - de, hi - de, hi - de -

Interlude

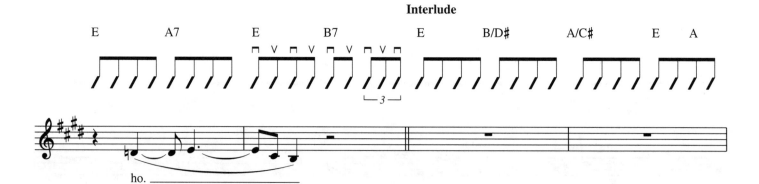

ho. _____

D.S. al Coda

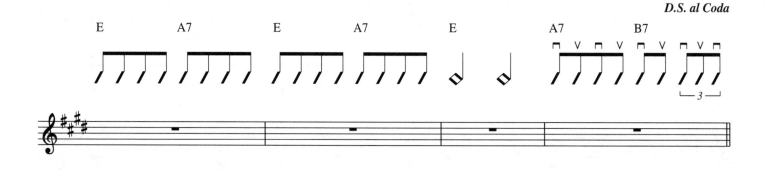

✠ **Coda**

Outro-Chorus

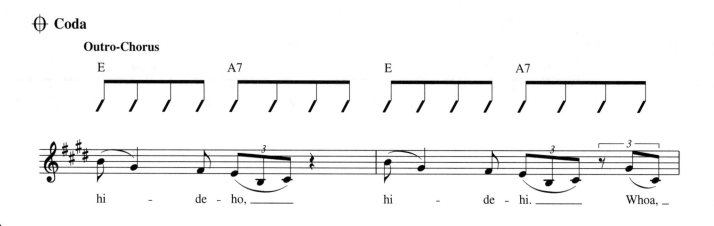

hi - de - ho, _____ hi - de - hi. _____ Whoa, _

Additional Lyrics

2. Once I met the devil,
   He was mighty slick.
   Tempted me with worldly goods,
   Said I could have my pick.
   But when he laid the paper on me,
   And showed me where to sign,
   I said, "Thank you very kindly
   But I'm in too great a need of mine."

I Feel the Earth Move

Words and Music by Carole King

your face, _____ mel-low as the month of ___ May. ___ Oh, _____ dar-

- lin', ___ I can't stand ___ it when you look at me that a way. _

D.S. al Coda 1   ⊕ **Coda 1**

_____ I feel the

Piano/Guitar Solo

4.   **Verse**

2. Ooh, _ dar - lin', _ when you're near _ me _____ and you ten - der-ly call my _ name, _

It's Too Late

Words by Toni Stern
Music by Carole King

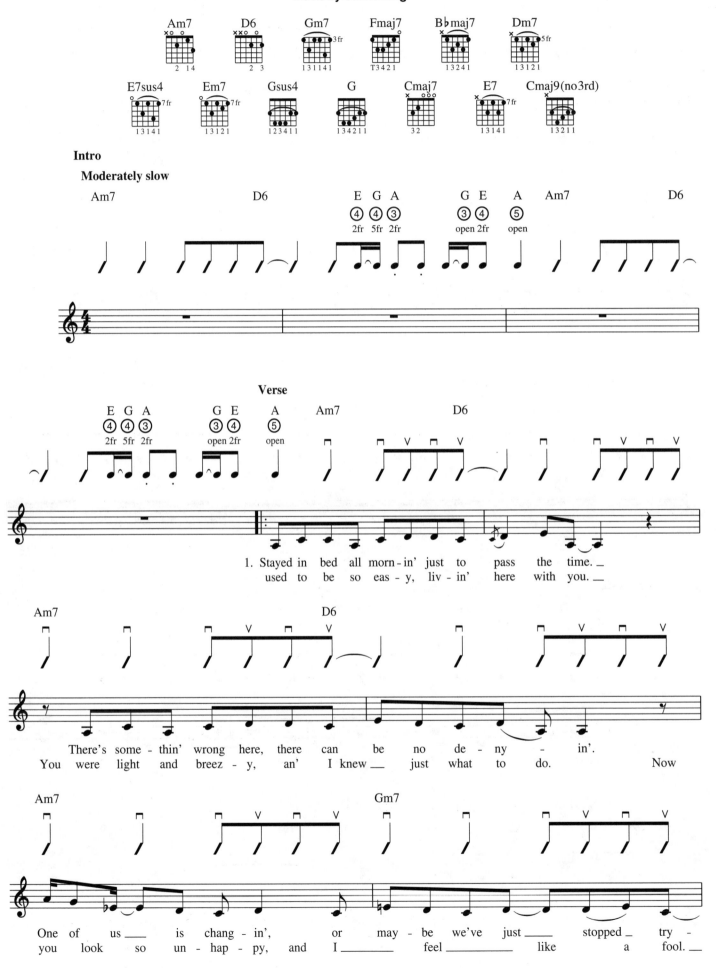

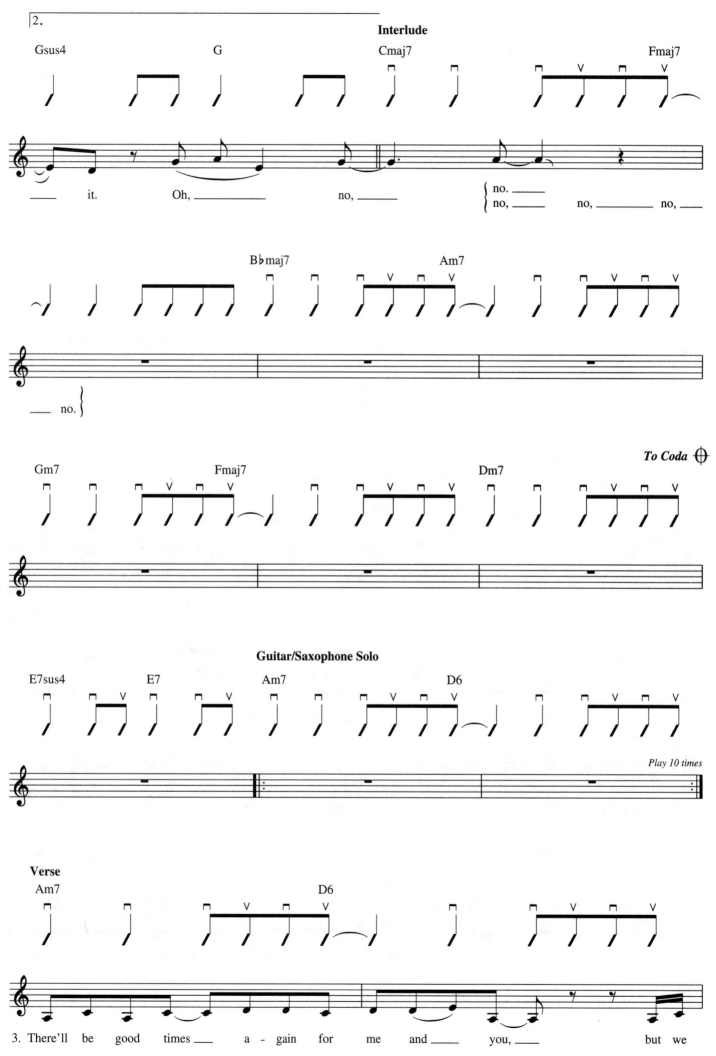

2.

Interlude

Gsus4   G   Cmaj7   Fmaj7

_____ it. Oh, _____ no, _____

{ no. _____
{ no, _____ no, _____ no, _____

B♭maj7   Am7

_____ no. }

To Coda ⊕

Gm7   Fmaj7   Dm7

Guitar/Saxophone Solo

E7sus4   E7   Am7   D6

Play 10 times

Verse

Am7   D6

3. There'll be good times _____ a - gain for me and _____ you, _____ but we

Jazzman

Words and Music by Carole King and David Palmer

Lift me, won't you lift me a-bove ___ the old rou-tine? Make it nice, ___ play it clean, ___ jazz - man. ___

Play 3 times

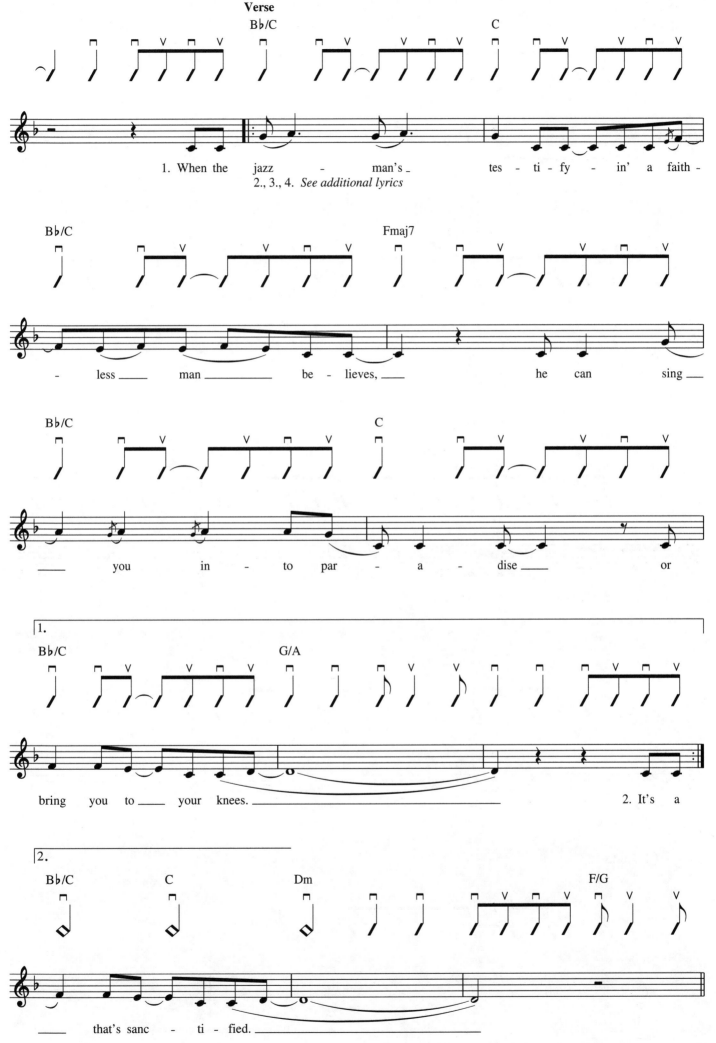

Verse

1. When the jazz — man's — tes - ti - fy - in' a faith -
2., 3., 4. *See additional lyrics*

- less — man — be - lieves, — he can sing —

— you in - to par - a - dise — or

1.

bring you to — your knees. — 2. It's a

2.

— that's sanc - ti - fied. —

Chorus

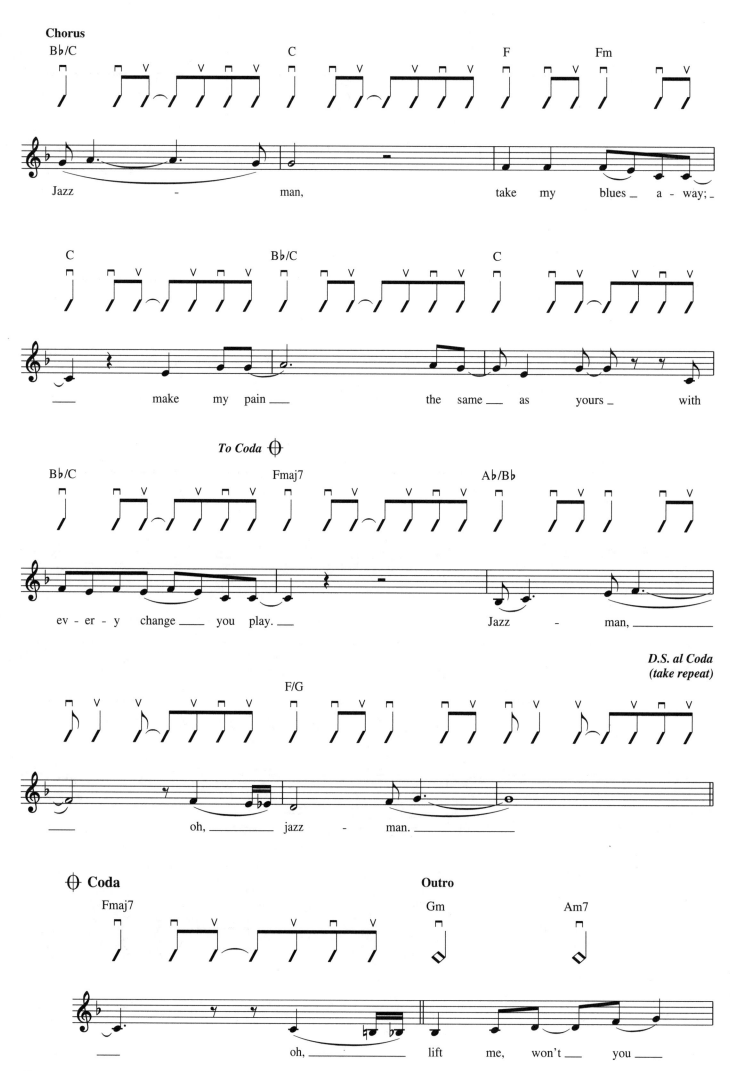

lift   me   with   ev - 'ry   turn - a - round; __

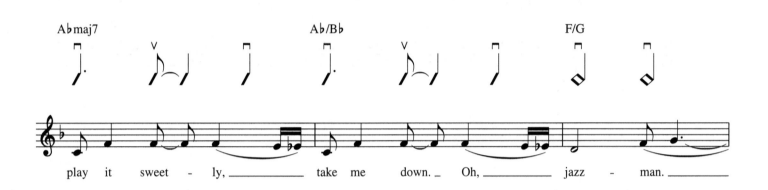

play   it   sweet - ly, _____   take   me   down. __   Oh, _____   jazz - man. _____

Play 7 times and fade

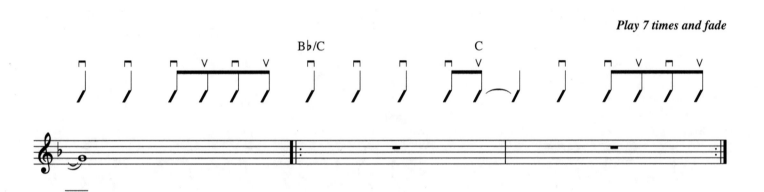

Additional Lyrics

2. It's a gospel kind of feelin',
   A touch of Georgia slide.
   A song of pure revival,
   And a style that's sanctified.

3. When the jazzman's signifyin',
   And the band is windin' low,
   It's the late night side of mornin',
   In the darkness of his soul.

4. He can fill the room with sadness,
   As he fills his horn with tears.
   He can cry like a fallen angel,
   When risin' time is near.

Nightingale

Words and Music by Carole King and David Palmer

seeks _____ the shel - tered nest.
_____ of his ___ suc - cess.

Like the sail - or's _____ lost ___ hor - i -
Those spot - light sha - dows, _____ how they lured _

- zon, _____ he needs _____
___ him _____ and took him _____

_____ some - place _ to rest. The
___ like all ___ the rest. But

Pre-Chorus

songs that he's ___ been ___ sing - in' _____ no _____ long - er ___ make much sense,
that old _ dream _ don't _ look ___ good _ now, ___ no it don't seem _ quite the same.

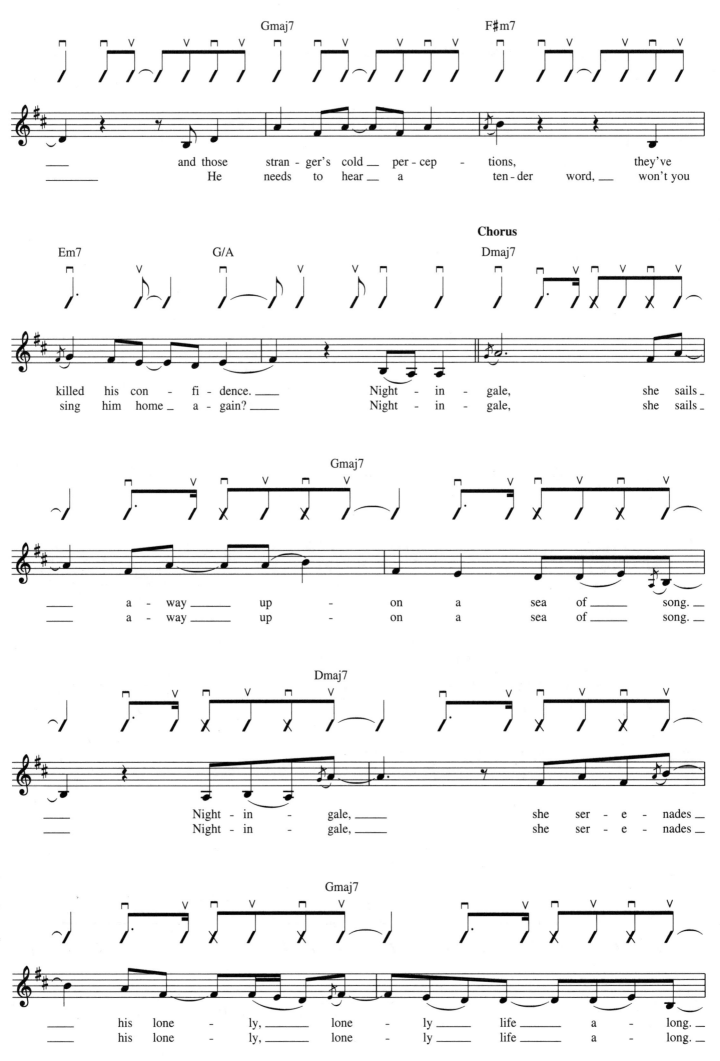

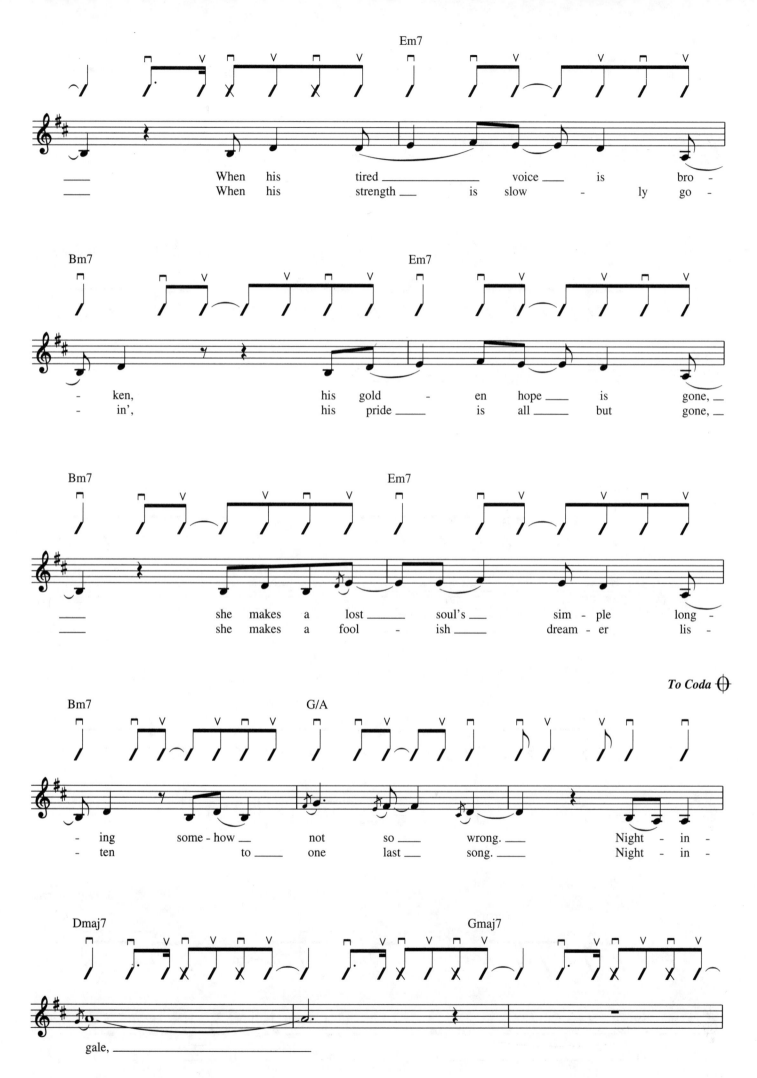

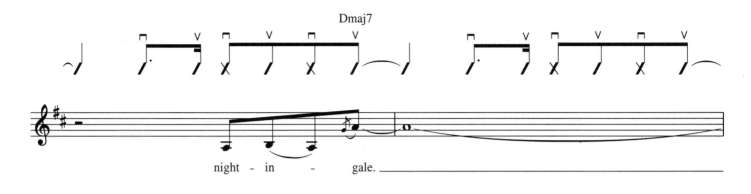

night - in - gale. _____

D.S. al Coda

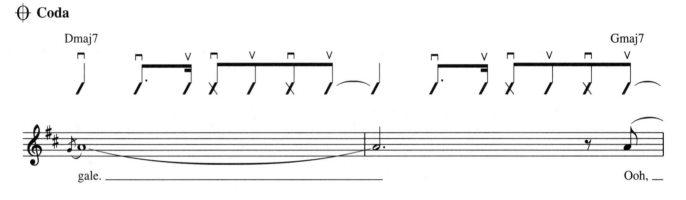

_____ 2. He was

Coda

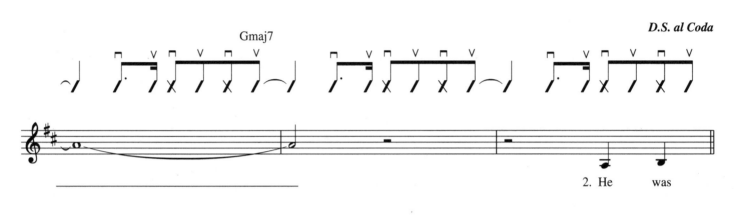

gale. _____ Ooh, __

Outro

_____ sing __ sweet __ night-in - gale. _____

Repeat and fade

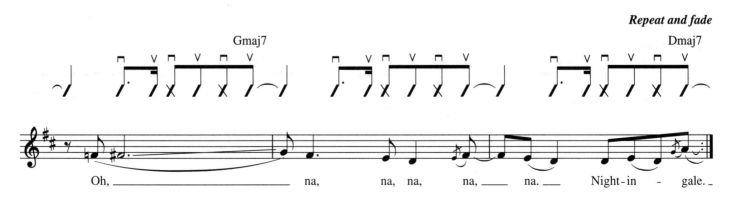

Oh, _____ na, na, na, na, __ na. __ Night-in - gale. __

So Far Away

Words and Music by Carole King

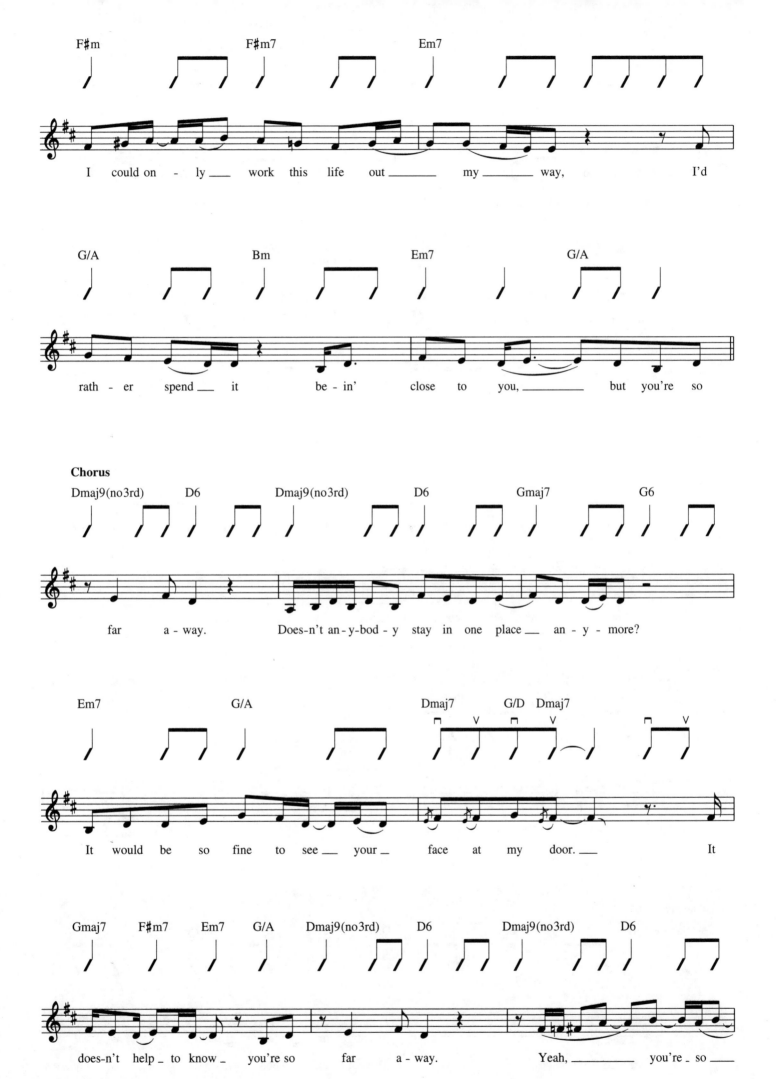

Verse

far ___ a - way. ___ 2. Trav - el - in' a - round sure gets me down _ and

lone - ly. _ Noth - in' else to do ___ but close my _ mind. _ I

sure ___ hope the road _ don't come to ___ own ___ me. There's

so man - y dreams _ I've yet to find. _____ But you're so

Chorus

far ___ a - way. Does - n't an - y - bod - y stay in one place _

Only Love Is Real

Words and Music by Carole King

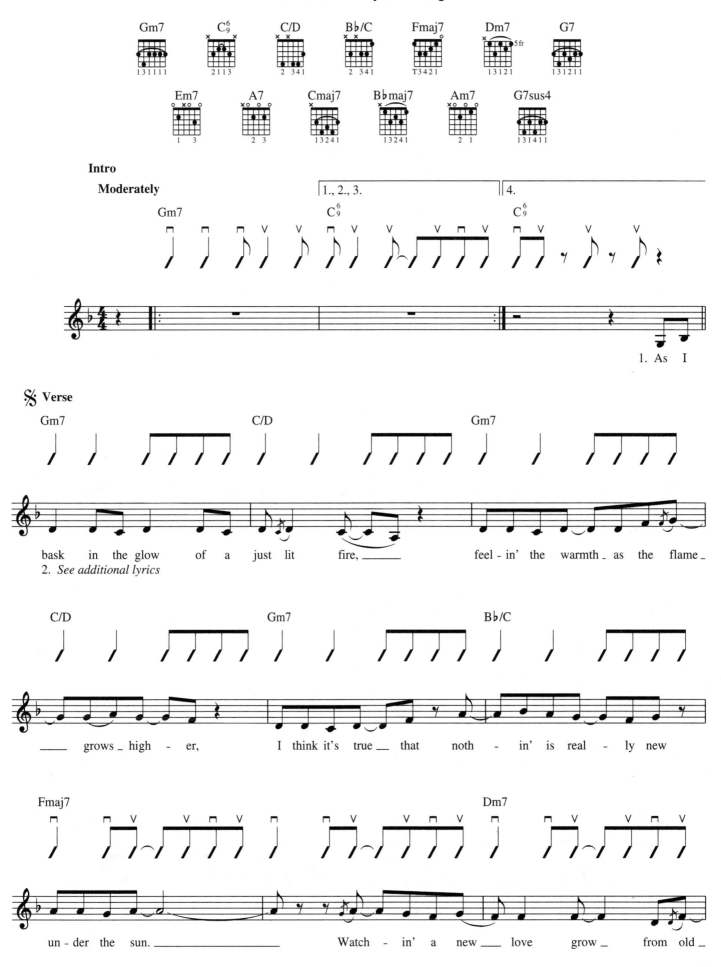

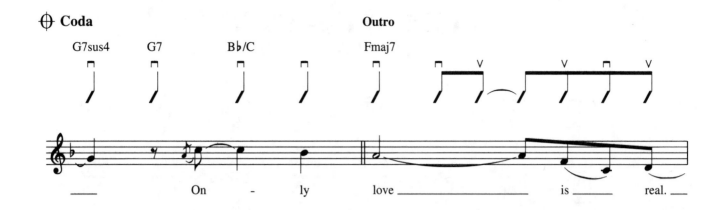

Coda

Outro

Outro

Repeat and fade

Additional Lyrics

2. Childhood dreams like muddy waters,
   Flowing through me to my son and daughters.
   Ev'rything I ever thought is confirmed as truth to me.
   Even as I see the way that I want to go now,
   Still, I wish I had known what I know now.
   Maybe I could have spared you givin' your youth to me.

Out in the Cold

Words and Music by Carole King

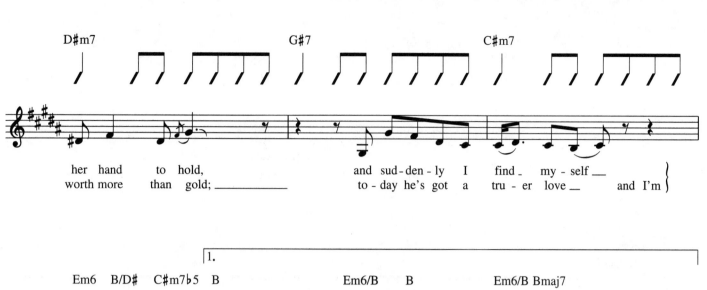

her hand   to hold,   and sud-den-ly I   find__ my-self __
worth more   than gold; _____   to-day he's got a   tru-er love __   and I'm

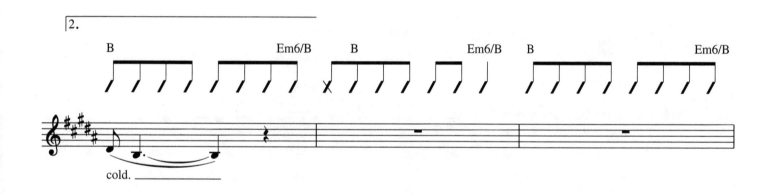

out   in __   the   cold. _____

cold. _____

Bridge

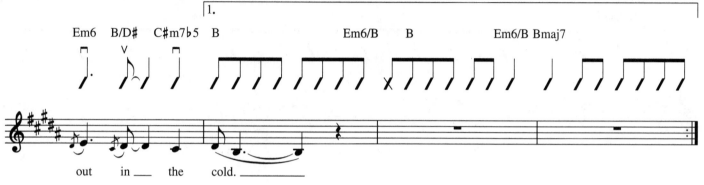

I   had   a love __ warm - er than fi - re, __

but I lis-tened to my __ de - si - re.   Now yes-ter-day's dreams   are to-

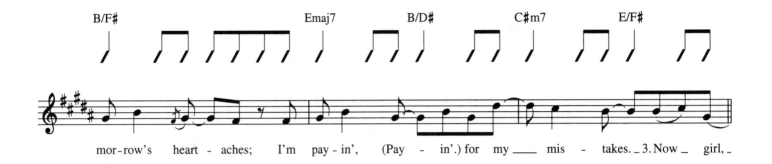

mor-row's heart-aches; I'm pay-in', (Pay - in'.) for my ___ mis - takes. _ 3. Now _ girl, _

Verse

___ take a tip from one __ who __ knows; _____

if you o - pen up a new door, you may _____ find _ the old _

___ one's closed. _ So be true to your good _ man,

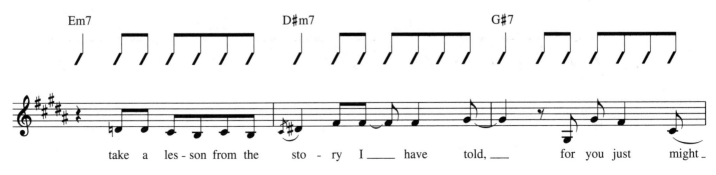

take a les - son from the sto - ry I __ have told, __ for you just might _

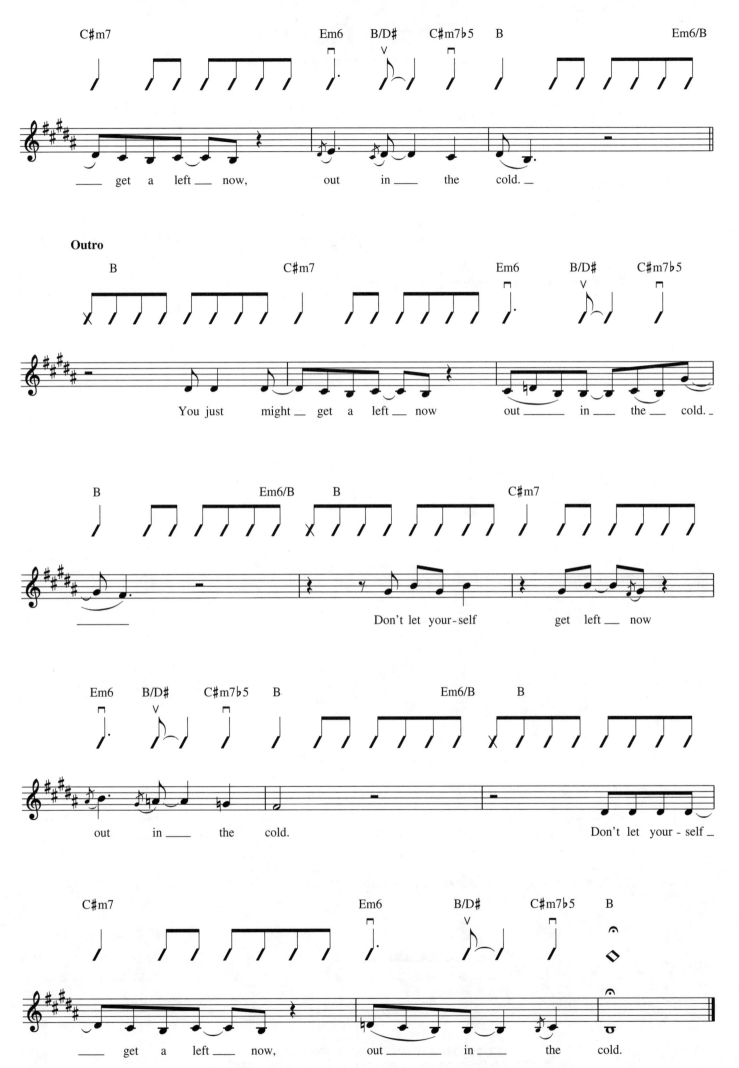

Outro

Really Rosy

Words and Music by Carole King and Maurice Sendak

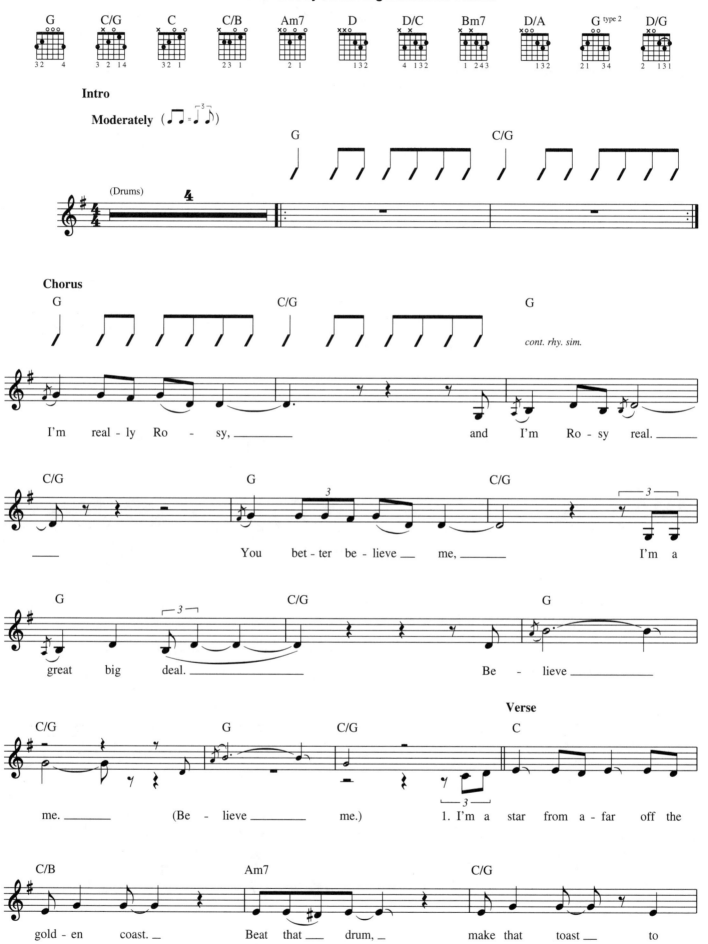

Smackwater Jack

Words and Music by Gerry Goffin and Carole King

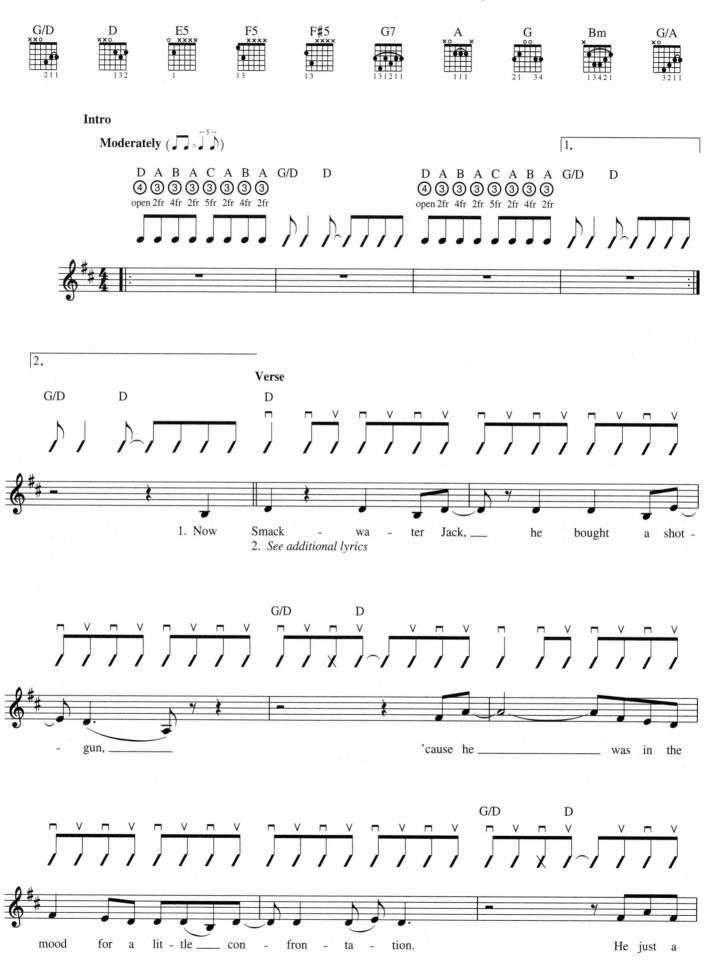

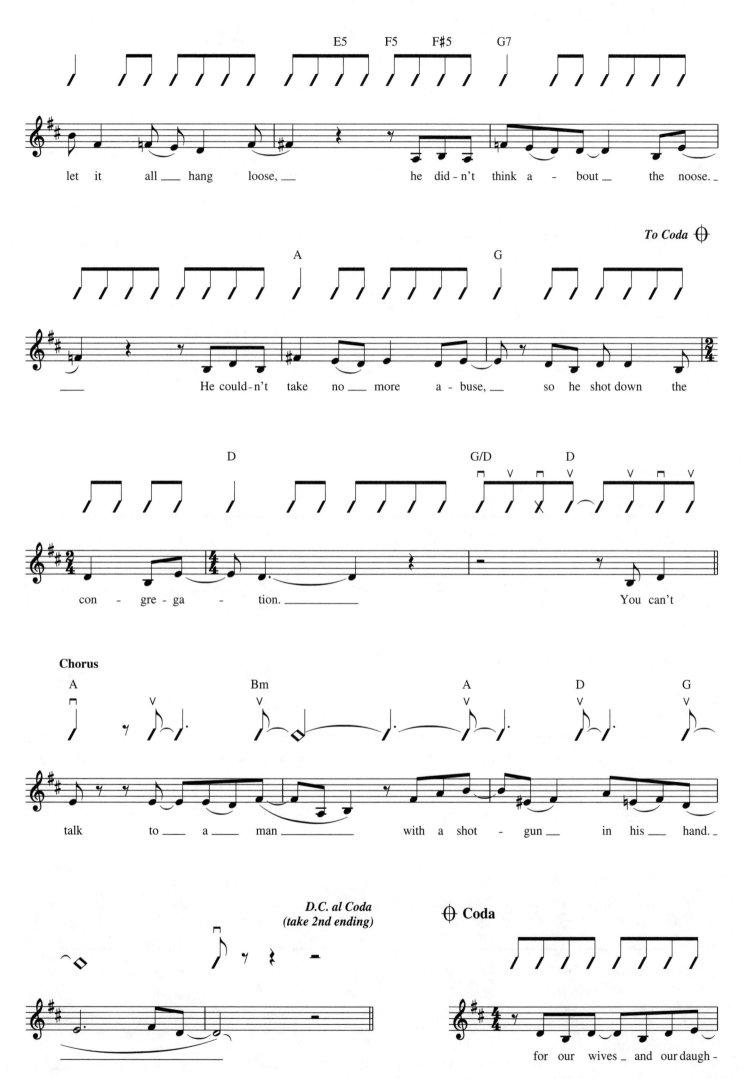

let it all ___ hang loose, ___ he did-n't think a - bout ___ the noose. ___

To Coda ⊕

___ He could-n't take no ___ more a - buse, ___ so he shot down the

con - gre - ga - tion. _____ You can't

Chorus

talk to ___ a ___ man _____ with a shot - gun ___ in his ___ hand. ___

D.C. al Coda
(take 2nd ending)

⊕ **Coda**

for our wives _ and our daugh -

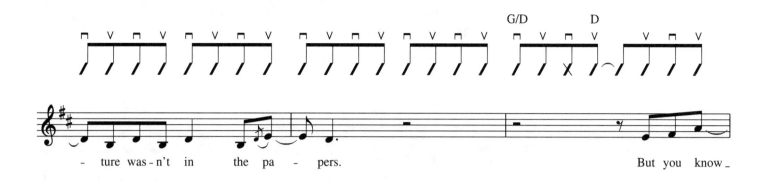

- ture was-n't in the pa - pers.   But you know

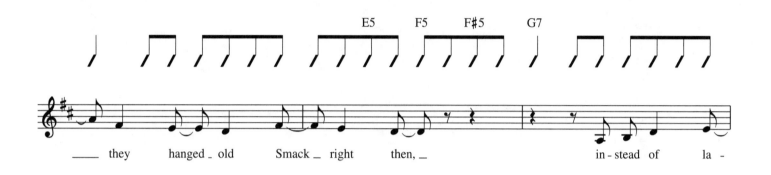

___ they hanged ___ old Smack ___ right then, ___   in - stead of la -

- ter.   You know the peo - ple ___ were ___ quite pleased, ___

___ 'cause the out - law ___ had ___ been siezed. _____ And on the

whole ___ it a was a ver - y good year _____ for the un - der - tak -

Outro

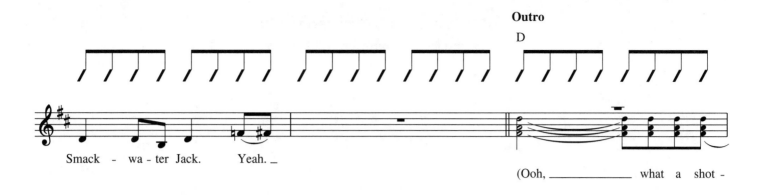

Smack - wa - ter Jack. Yeah. _

(Ooh, _____ what a shot -

cont. rhy. sim.

- gun.) Talk - ing 'bout a Smack - wa - ter Jack. Ah. (Ooh! _____

Talk - ing 'bout Jack and his shot - gun. Talk - ing 'bout Smack. _

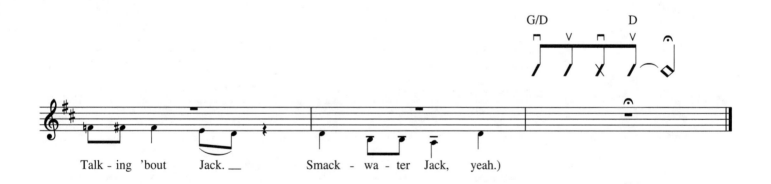

Talk - ing 'bout Jack. _ Smack - wa - ter Jack, yeah.)

Additional Lyrics

2. Now Big Jim, the chief, stood for law and order.
   He called for the guard to come and surround the border.
   Now from his bulldog mouth, as he lead the posse south,
   Came the cry, "We've got to ride to clean up the streets for our wives and our daughters."

65

Sweet Seasons

Words and Music by Carole King and Toni Stern

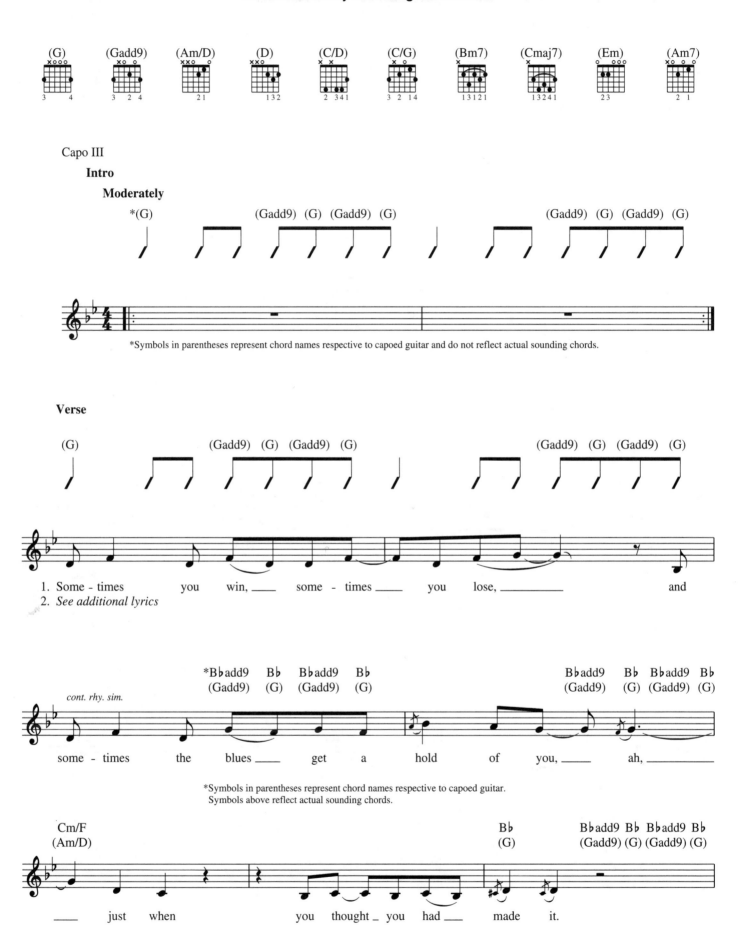

Capo III

Intro

Moderately

*Symbols in parentheses represent chord names respective to capoed guitar and do not reflect actual sounding chords.

Verse

1. Some - times you win, ___ some - times ___ you lose, ___ and
2. *See additional lyrics*

some - times the blues ___ get a hold of you, ___ ah, ___

*Symbols in parentheses represent chord names respective to capoed guitar.
Symbols above reflect actual sounding chords.

___ just when you thought ___ you had ___ made it.

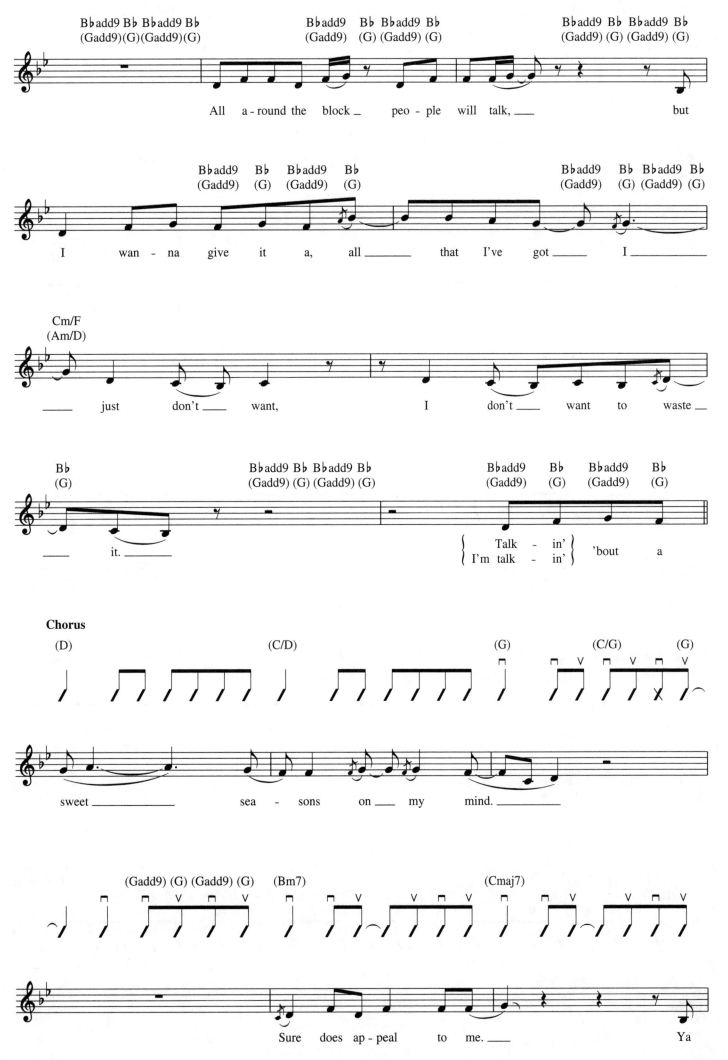

Additional Lyrics

2. Sometimes you win, sometimes you lose,
   Then most times you choose between the two,
   Ah, wonderin', wonderin' if you have made it.
   But I'll have some kids and make my plans,
   And I'll watch the seasons runnin' away,
   And I'll build me a life in the open,
   A life in the country.

69

Tapestry

Words and Music by Carole King

71

cer - tain - ty, as if he did - n't know just what he was there ___ for, ___ or ___ where he ought to go. ___

___ Once he reached ___ for some - thing ___ gold - en, hang - ing from a tree, ___ and his hand came down

D.S. al Coda

emp - ty.

Coda

Verse

well. 5. As I ___ watched in sor - row, there sud - den - ly ___ ap - peared ___ a fig - ure, ___ gray and ghost - ly, be - neath ___ a flow - ing beard. ___ In

times   of   deep-est   dark   -   ness, ___   I've   seen ___ him   dressed   in

black.   Now   my   tap - es - try's   un - rav - el - ing,   he's

come ___   to take   me   back.   He's   come ___   to take   me

back.

Outro

A tempo

Where You Lead

Words and Music by Carole King and Toni Stern

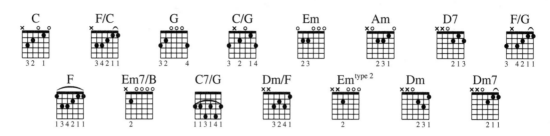

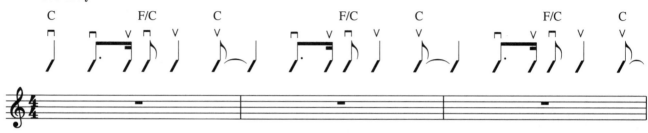

Intro

Moderately

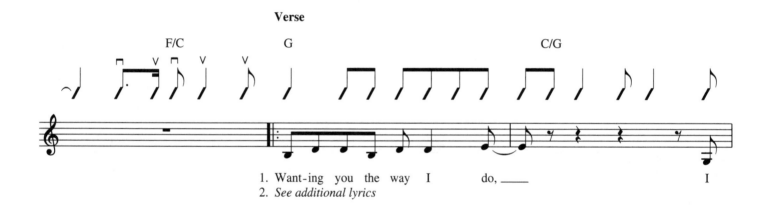

1. Want-ing you the way I do, _____ I
2. *See additional lyrics*

on - ly want to be with _ you. _____ And I would go _____ to the ends _

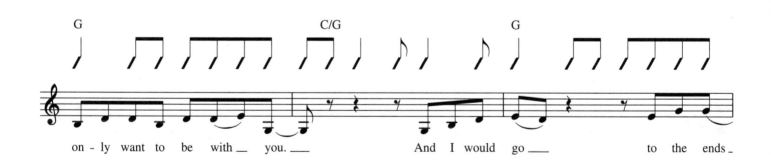

_____ of the earth, 'cause _ dar - lin' to me that's what you're worth. _ Where you lead _____

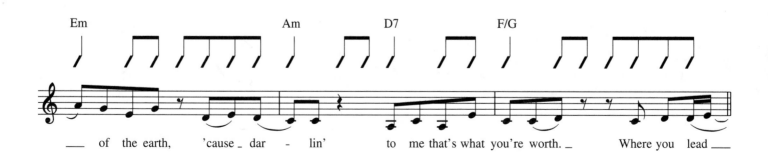

Chorus

I nev - er thought I could get ___ sat - is - fac - - tion

from just one ___ man, _____ but if an - y - one _____ can keep ___

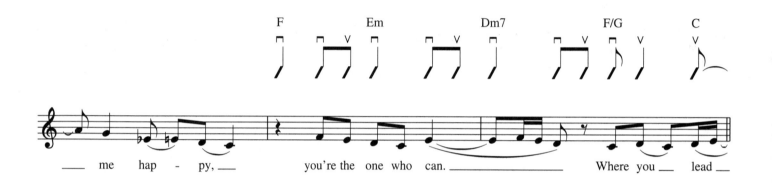

___ me hap - py, ___ you're the one who can. _____ Where you ___ lead ___

Chorus

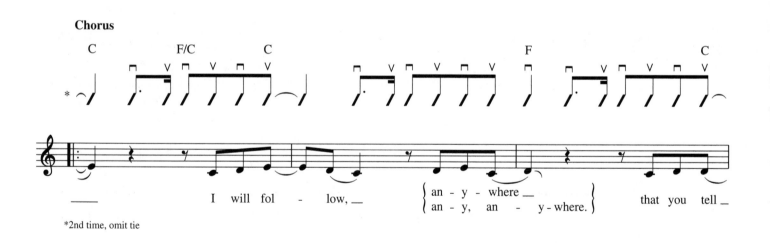

*___ I will fol - low, ___ { an - y - where ___ / an - y, an - y - where. } that you tell ___

*2nd time, omit tie

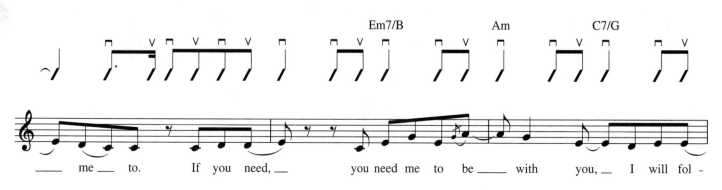

___ me ___ to. If you need, ___ you need me to be ___ with you, ___ I will fol -

Additional Lyrics

2. If you're out on the road,
   Feelin' lonely and so cold,
   All you have to do is call my name
   And I'll be there on the next train.

Will You Love Me Tomorrow
(Will You Still Love Me Tomorrow)

Words and Music by Gerry Goffin and Carole King

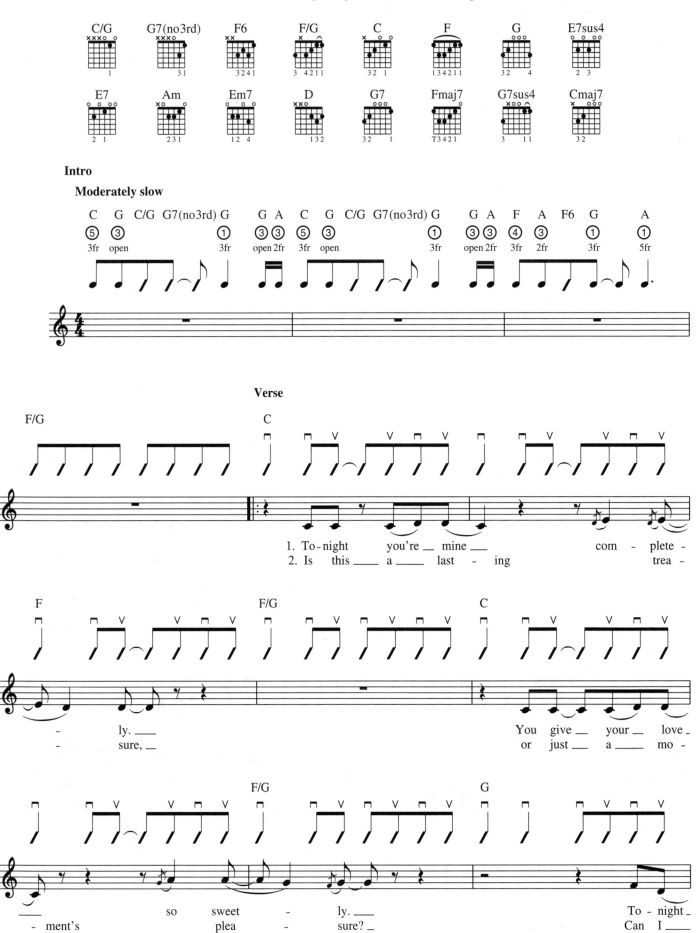

the light _____ of ___ love ___ is in your ___ eyes. _____
be - lieve _____ the ___ mag - ic of your ___ sighs? _____

But will you love ___ me to - mor -
Will you still love ___ me to - mor -

1. **2.**

- row?
- row?

Bridge

cont. rhy. sim.

To - night with words ___ un - spok - en, ___

you say that I'm _____ the on - ly one. ___

You've Got a Friend

Words and Music by Carole King

*Symbols in parentheses represent chord names respective to capoed guitar and do not reflect actual sounding chords.

Bridge

85

Chorus

(C/D)   (D)   (G)

don't you let ___ them. _____ You just call ___ out my ___ name, ___

(C)

and you know ___ wher - ev - er I am, ___ I'll ___ come run -

(G) (Gadd9) (G) (Gadd9) (G)   (Gsus4 type 2) (G)   (C/D)

- nin' a - run - nin', yeah, ___ yeah, _____ to see you a - gain. ___

(G)   (Gmaj9)

Win - ter, spring, sum - mer or fall, _____

(C)   (Em)   (G7)   (Cmaj7)   (Bm7)

all you have to do is call, _____ and I'll be _____ there, _ yes, I ___ will. _____

*Symbols in parentheses represent chord names respective to capoed guitar.
Symbols above reflect actual sounding chords.

Additional Lyrics

2. If the sky above you,
   Grows dark and full of clouds,
   And that old north wind begins to blow;
   Keep your head together,
   And call my name out loud.
   Soon you'll hear me knockin' at your door.